# A Synopsis

# and Personal Appraisal

# of the Theology of

# Thomas F. Torrance

## James A. Fowler

**A Synopsis and Personal Appraisal
of the Theology of T.F. Torrance**

James A. Fowler

©2017 by James A. Fowler

ISBN 978-1-929541-57-7

*Printed in the United States of America*

**C.I.Y. Publishing**
P.O. Box 1822
Fallbrook, CA 92088
www.Christinyou.net

# A Synopsis and Personal Appraisal of the Theology of Thomas F. Torrance:

© 2017 by James A. Fowler

## Biographical information

Thomas Forsyth Torrance was born in Chengdu, Szechuan, China, August 30, 1913, the first son of missionary parents, Thomas and Annie (better known as "Betty") Torrance, who ministered under the auspices of the China Inland Mission. (Having gone to China in 1897, the elder Tom Torrance likely was acquainted with J. Hudson Taylor, the founder of the CIM, who died in China in 1905.) The elder Tom Torrance later served with the American Bible Society in China for 23 years. T.F. Torrance had two brothers, James and David, and three sisters, Mary, Grace, and Margaret. His early education took place in China, where he learned the Mandarin language. In 1927, when Tom was 13 years old, the family returned to Scotland due to a deteriorating political situation, while his father returned to China for 7 more years. Tom took an MA degree in the Greek and Latin Classics and philosophy at the Univ. of Edinburgh, and subsequently completed a B.D. degree in Christian theology from New College, Edinburgh. At the recommendation of his professor H.R. Macintosh, he went on to pursue a Th.D. degree under Karl Barth in Basel, Switzerland, writing his dissertation on "The Doctrine of Grace in the Apostolic Fathers." He was later asked to assume the chair of theology as successor to Karl Barth at Basel, but declined.

On one occasion, in 1936, when Torrance went to the Middle East to study Biblical languages and archaeology, he survived a poisoned drink, had a revolver thrust at him when an Arab accused him of being a Jew, and then was arrested in Iraq for being a spy. He was transported to Baghdad, sentenced to death, but was eventually deported to Syria. After that ordeal he taught theology for one year at Auburn University in the United States in 1938,39, but returned to Scotland because his country was threatened with war. He volunteered and served as a chaplain in Italy, where a young, dying soldier plaintively asked him, "Is God the same as Jesus?" That question haunted him, for he realized that there was a serious bifurcation between the way people viewed God and the way people viewed Jesus in the teaching of the church – a serious Trinitarian and Christological breakdown.

After the war T. F. Torrance ministered at three different parishes in the Church of Scotland, prior to being invited to assume the chair of Church History at New College, Univ. of Edinburgh. Two years later, in 1952, he transferred to the chair of Christian Dogmatics at New College, where he lectured as professor for 27 years. His brother, James Torrance joined him as a lecturer at New College, until he was invited to become the chair of theology at the University of Aberdeen, Scotland. During his professorship at New College Tom founded the highly respected *Scottish Journal of Theology*, translated the 6 million word *Church Dogmatics* of Karl Barth from German to English (along with G.W. Bromiley), and retranslated *Calvin's Commentaries* from Latin into English (with the assistance of his brother, David). His book entitled *Theological Science*, published in 1969 resulted in his being awarded the prestigious Templeton Prize for Progress in Religion in 1978.

T.F. Torrance is renowned for his integrative studies in the philosophical epistemology of science and theology, and it is in consonance with those methodological studies that Torrance developed his distinctive emphases in his Dogmatic Theology. The accolades of the work of T.F.

Torrance have been many, and he is touted by some as "the greatest Scottish theologian of all time," while others have regarded him as the "greatest English-speaking theologian of the twentieth century."

It was my privilege to sit under the theological tutelage of T.F. Torrance and his brother J.B. Torrance when I matriculated into a masters degree program in Dogmatic Theology at New College Seminary, University of Edinburgh, Scotland in 1968. Although that degree program was not completed, I did have the opportunity to soak up an abundance of theological data that I was only able to assimilate and evaluate in later years. T.F. Torrance would often hand out extensive mimeographed notes of his lectures, which I have retained to this day, but they have conveniently been recently edited and published by his nephew, Robert T. Walker, in two volumes, *Incarnation* (2008) and *Atonement* (2009).

After his retirement from the University of Edinburgh, T.F. Torrance was involved in a symposium think-tank relating science with Christianity at Princeton University. His son, Ian Torrance, later became president of Princeton, University. Tom Torrance suffered a debilitating stroke in 2003, and graduated to glory on December 2, 2007.

The theological thought of T.F. Torrance has experienced a remarkable renaissance in the twenty-first century. The Thomas F. Torrance Theological Fellowship was founded in 2004, and that organization publishes a theological journal called *Participatio*.

The theological structures articulated by TF Torrance in the latter part of the 20th century, are continuing to be expounded in the 21st century by the many students and associates that he influenced, and as a consequence we are observing the ground-swell of a call for a radical renewal of Christian theological thinking.

Many theological professors in major theological schools around our country and the world subscribe to and are teaching theology that has its foundation in the thought of TF Torrance. I have no doubt that the propagation of the thought of T.F. Torrance will increase exponentially in the coming decades. Professors are teaching those who will be teaching others all the way down to the Christian people in the pews of the churches. The number of doctoral dissertations in theology dealing with the theology of TFT is phenomenal. The number of secondary source materials being published concerning the theology of TFT is burgeoning. The thought of TFT may become more pronounced than that of Karl Barth, his theological mentor, at least in the English-speaking theological world.

Since the voluminous writings of T.F. Torrance cannot be thoroughly or even properly analyzed in the confines of such an introduction and personal analysis as is being attempted here, all I can do is to briefly touch on a few of the major categories of his thought, attempting to simplify them in my own words, because admittedly TF Torrance was not easy to comprehend, either in his lectures or in his writings.

In this severely limited overview, I intend to consider some of the distinctive aspects of **Christology** that flow from his Trinitarian theology. This will necessarily involve the **soteriological** implications of how the divine-human God-man, Jesus, effected salvation for all mankind by Who He was and what He did. Torrance believed that Christology and soteriology were integrally united and could not be separated. Who Jesus *was* and *is* as the eternal divine-human God-man constitutes the entirety of what He *did* and *does*, in Torrance's theological understanding.

## Distinctives of the Theology of TF Torrance

TF Torrance regarded the Nicene *homoousion* and the Chalcedonian "hypostatic union" as the inner matrix of God's Self-revelation, and he constructed his theology upon these two pillars of what he called "God's Self-disclosure Model." Upon these foundational tenets TF Torrance set out to build his theological edifice.

The "twin towers" of TFTs thought might be explained as the **"vicarious humanity"** of Jesus and the **"incarnational atonement"** of all humanity effected by Christ's "vicarious humanity." They are complementary to one another, and cannot be separated. Incarnational redemption, justification and reconciliation (at-one-ment) conjoined with the assumption and sanctification of humanity in the "vicarious humanity" of Jesus.

Affirming the conclusions and declarations of the early councils of the Church, TFT grounds his Trinitarian thought in the *mia ousia, treis hypostaseis* (one Being, three Persons) of the Cappadocian Fathers, and constructs his Christological thought by keying off of the Nicene statement of Jesus' being *homoousion to Patri* (one Being with the Father). But it is particularly the Chalcedonian construct of the "hypostatic union" expressed in *dia physein, mia hypostasis* (two natures, one person) that is the springboard for Torrance's expanded theological system.

TFT made constant reference to the Athanasian formulation of Trinitarian and Christological thought stated in the Nicene Creed (325). Athanasius insisted that the Christian understanding of the person of Jesus Christ be explained in terms of the Greek word *homoousion*. *Homoousion* is a combination of two other Greek words, *homo*, meaning "same" (it is familiar today in the word "*homo*sexual") and the second Greek word is *ousia*, meaning "being" (it is used in the transliterated English word "parousia," meaning "to *be* present," which in its biblical meaning pertains to the "second coming" of Christ, when He is *present* in visible *Being* again). The one opposing Athanasius at the Council of Nicea (325) was Arius, who insisted that Jesus was *anomoousios* (not the same being as the Father), or *homoiousios* (of merely similar being with the Father) or *anomoiousios* (not even similar to the Father). Athanasius won the argument at the Council of Nicea, with the opinions of Arius being condemned, and the Nicene Creed used the word *homoousion* to explain that Jesus was *homoousios to Patri*, of one Being with the Father, for Jesus Himself had said, "I and the Father are one" (John 10:30), and such unity of essence was determined to be foundational to the distinctive Christian understanding of God.

The idea of "hypostatic union" as developed at the Council of Chalcedon (A.D. 451) was also foundational to TFT's theological system. The "hypostatic union" of the deity and humanity of Jesus Christ was the clarification of Christology. As early as A.D. 251, Origen had defined God as "one genus of *ousia*, while being three, distinct species of *hypostasis*." It wasn't easy for the early Christian thinkers to attempt to find words to explain the uniqueness of the Christian understanding of God and the Person of Jesus Christ. The Greek word *hypostatis*, literally meant "to stand under," but linguistically referred to the "underpinning" or foundational existence of something, and was used in Trinitarian thought in the phrase, "one Being (*ousia*) in three (*hypostases*) substances, subsistences, existences or individuals." When the Greek word *hypostasis* was translated into the Latin as *persona* the standard Christian expression for the Triune God became "three persons in one Being." The problem this presented was complicated by the fact that the Latin *persona* was used of a masked actor on the theatre stage who was taking on the persona of another, and this was certainly not what Christian thinkers were attempting to project upon the personages of the tri-fold God.

Early Christological discussions also chose to use this Greek word *hypostasis* in reference to the union of deity and humanity in Jesus Christ. The Chalcedonian Creed formulated at the Council of Chalcedon in AD 451 declared that Jesus was comprised of two natures (Greek word *phusis*), deity and humanity, in one *hypostasis* (subsistence, individual) or person (to use the Latin equivalent *persona*). This came to be known as the "hypostatic union" of the Person of Jesus Christ. To this day the idea of "two natures" in the Person of Jesus provides difficulty, for this is subsequently used to justify the idea of "two natures" in the Christian, even though they are used in reference to entirely different realities. The Oriental Orthodox churches of the East rejected the Chalcedonian formulation of "hypostatic union" and charged the Western churches with *dyophysitism* (two naturism), while they, in turn, were charged with *monophysitism* (one naturism) by the Western church.

I share this rather convoluted synopsis of word origins and early theological formulations to demonstrate Torrance's commitment to the early creedal formulations of Christian doctrine to which he made constant reference. In fact, Torrance took the Nicean and Chalcedonian constructs of *homoousion* and hypostatic union and made these the linchpins of his subsequent Christological and soteriological system.

From these early formulations TFT develops a theology that seems to have two primary pivot points that are so intertwined as to be incapable of separation. These two emphases I have identified as "the vicarious humanity of Jesus" and "incarnational atonement."

7

The "hypostatic union" of divinity and humanity in Jesus is the *primary* springboard of Torrances' theological construct. "If Jesus Christ the incarnate Son is not true God from true God, then we are not saved, for it is only God who can save; but if Jesus Christ is not truly man, then salvation does not touch our human existence and condition." (TFT *Mediation* 146-149)

From the Chalcedonian expression of the "hypostatic union" of divinity and humanity in the person of Jesus Christ, TFT goes on to formulate the doctrine of the "vicarious humanity" of Jesus for, on behalf of, and in place of all humanity. The word "vicarious" has long been utilized in Christian thought, meaning to substitute, to speak and act on behalf of another, or in place of another. Historically, the term has been used to refer to the "vicarious death" of Jesus, explaining that Jesus was the only viable sinless substitute whose sacrificial death could suffice to take the death consequences of sin on behalf of fallen, sinful humanity.

Torrance views the "vicarious humanity" of Jesus as a direct correlate of the "hypostatic union" first articulated at Chalcedon, emphasizing that in the incarnation of the person of Jesus, the divine-human mediator, Jesus brings God to man and man to God.

But the question must be asked whether TFT's expansion and extension of the "hypostatic union" to universally include the representation and replacement of all human beings, all humanity, in the "incarnational redemption and atonement" of Jesus' birth as the God-man is a legitimate extension from the particular to the universal – or does this go beyond the intent of Chalcedon?

## Analysis and Evaluation of Torrance's Thought

As attention is now turned to the personal analysis and evaluation of TFT's thought, I will be using some admittedly arbitrary categories to formulate and explain the structure of his thought. We do not want to misrepresent TFT, nor do we want to superimpose upon TFT's thought any concepts or ideas that are not intrinsic to what he has explicated.

The following diagram of "The Distinctives of the Theology of T.F. Torrance" is the author's personal attempt to diagrammatically illustrate the core of his thought. Bringing together the *homoousios* teaching of Nicea and the "hypostatic union" emphasis of Chalcedon, Torrance seeks to tie together "Who Jesus IS" and "What Jesus DOES," i.e. His Person and His work, thus bringing Christology and soteriology into a unified explanation via the tenets of the "vicarious humanity" of Jesus in correlation with the theological premise of "incarnational atonement."

### Distinctives of the Theology of T.F. Torrance

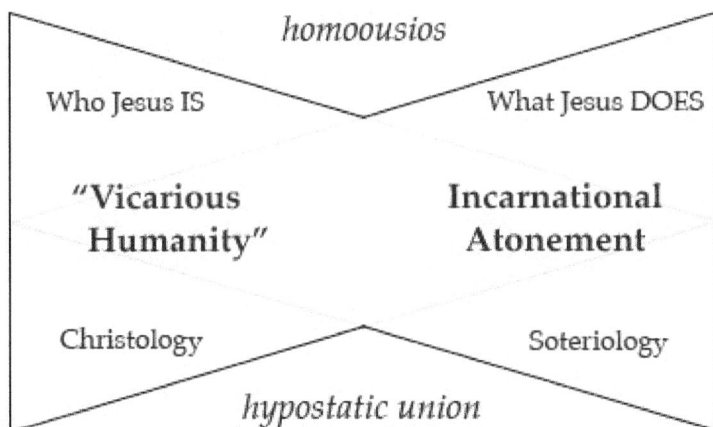

*homoousios*

Who Jesus IS     What Jesus DOES

"Vicarious Humanity"     Incarnational Atonement

Christology     Soteriology

*hypostatic union*

## Presuppositions in the Thought of T.F. Torrance

It should be instructive to consider some of the presuppositions that seem to exist in the theology of T.F. Torrance. To begin with we must note that Torrance has a real "ax to grind" concerning the "dualisms" that he perceives to have pervaded human thought based on the best of human reasoning. To counter such, he attempts to construct a holistic and unitary theological system that rejects all dualisms.

In his adamant reaction to *dualism*, T.F. Torrance tends to reject the perspective of dialectic that was much stronger in Karl Barth, especially in his earlier writings (ex. *Romans*), and that due to Karl Barth's appreciation of the Danish thinker, Soren Kierkegaard. Kierkegaard referred to the "infinite qualitative difference" between God and man, and Barth's explanation was that God was "wholly other" than man. Karl Barth was often described as a "dialectic theologian," but it is doubtful that T.F. Torrance would be so labeled, except in the Hegelian sense exemplified by his repetitive attempts to integrate dualistic ideas into a unitary theological structure – certainly not the balanced tension of the both/and dialectic that was evident in Kierkegaard and in the early writings of Barth. The dialectic of TFT is an Hegelian dialectic, rather than Kierkegaardian dialectic.

TFT was so intent on ferreting out dualism that sometimes he seemed to be finding dualism under every bush. TFT sees dualism everywhere he looks. All either-or dichotomies, and all both-and dialectics seem to be viewed as dualisms by TFT. Distinctions that have been made throughout the history of Christian theology are identified as "dualisms" by TFT. For example: the Person and work of Jesus Christ; incarnation and atonement; Christology and soteriology, revelation and reconciliation, justification and sanctification, grace and human freedom; divine agency and human agency. TFT seeks to bring them all together in one singular (some would say "monistic") event and act, with everything unified in the incarnation of Jesus Christ. It is not difficult to see why TFT has been charged with Christomonism, along with his mentor, Karl Barth.

In his reaction to the perceived dualisms, TFT attempted to construct a unitary theological construct (in like manner as Hegel attempted philosophically, and Einstein sought scientifically). TFT referred to this as a unitary and "holistic" theology.

A second presupposition that seems to be present in TFT's thinking is that all Jesus *does* is implicit in who He *IS* (the entirety of His *doing* is inherent in His *being*). This is developed in Torrance's thought in the explanation that who Jesus Christ **is** as God-man and Savior effects (not affects, but is the essential cause of) all that he **does** in salvation, reconciliation, union, etc. The "doing" of Jesus is implicit in His "Being," and His "Being" is integral to His "doing."

Although others have indicated, "God *does* what He *does*, because He *IS* who He *IS*," TFT takes it to another logical step, indicating that the action is implicit in the Being. i.e., because Jesus Christ exists as the divine-human mediator between God and man, the entire action of the mediation (redemption, justification, atonement, etc.) is accomplished by His very Being and existence, within the "hypostatic union" of His incarnation.

A third presupposition in the thought of TFT maintains his Reformed theological background in an objectification that discounts the individual subjective action of the human being.

Protestantism in general – Lutheranism, Calvinism, and most of the offshoots – has tended to emphasize an overly-objectified gospel. They have avoided any emphasis on the interiority of the personal and subjective relationship with the living Lord Jesus Christ. Although TFT challenges the legal and forensic factors of the Protestant objectification, he nonetheless retains a perspective of Christ's work that is almost exclusively objectified.

A fourth presupposition coincides with the third. TFT seems to begin his thinking with the premise of a divine determinism that diminishes human freedom of choice

TFT and his mentor, Karl Barth, both had their theological heritage in the Reformed theological tradition that accepted and advocated the Augustinian/Calvinist foundations of a "sovereign," deterministic God in a manner that disallowed, or at least severely diminished, the value and efficacy of any meaningful response on the part of an individual to God's redemptive and restorative work in Jesus Christ.

A fifth presupposition that should be noted is TF Torrance's tendency to engage in *a priori* epistemology, consistent with his overall approach of philosophical realism.

Having commenced with the ideas of *homoousios* and "hypostatic union," TFT builds on those premises with an *a priori* epistemology that postulates, hypothesizes, and speculates about the expanded implications of these foundational statements. He rejected this basis of epistemology in his consideration of the doctrine of God, but seems to utilize the same logical process in the extensions of the creedal statements of the early church. TFT seems to make the very kinds of projections and postulations in terms of Christology and soteriology that he eschewed in the Western development of Trinitarian theology proper.

**Extensions and Expansions of early Christian Creedal Statements in the Thought of T.F. Torrance**

It has previously been explained that TFT was keen to tie his thought to the early Christian theological articulations of the Christian faith. The question to be considered is whether he remains true and accurate to the early Christian statements, or whether he extends and expands the early creedal statements to meanings and teaching that were never intended by the original writers.

It is safe to say that the *homoousios* doctrine of early Christian teaching, from Nicea onward, is an important clarification in Christian thought. But the first of TFT's questionable extensions of early Christian thought comes as he attempts extend the *homoousios* of Nicean Christological and Trinitarian thought to apply to a unity of being between Triune Being and human being.
Torrance takes the creedal expression of Nicea and seeks to weld it with the Chalcedonian expression of hypostatic union, and then expands the implications to the whole of humanity. "Jesus Christ is *homoousios* with the Father as to His Godhead and *homoousios* with us as to his manhood."

TF Torrance attempts to extend the *homoousios* of the Father, Son, and Holy Spirit to include a recreation and recapitulation of humanity whereby all human beings partake and participate in the "same being" of the Triune God. Torrance often quotes the early church writers who said, "Christ became man, that we might become God," and many writers have noted the similarity of TFT's thought to the *theosis* teaching of the Eastern church.

A second extension and expansion of early Christian thought is evident in Torrance's utilization of the concept of *perichoresis* that was used by early Christian thinkers to refer to the essential participation of the Persons of the

13

Trinity. Torrance extends the meaning of *perichoresis* to refer to the essential participation of the Triune God and all humanity.

The word *perichoresis* was used by the Cappadocian Fathers, and was later used in both Christological and Trinitarian discussions. TFT (and perhaps more explicitly his brother, JBT) seeks to extend the concept to the universal interpenetration of all humanity with the persons of the Trinity. In terms of our recreated human "being" we can now exist and move around in the same space or place with the Father, Son, and Holy Spirit. This becomes a form of absorption or comingling of man with deity, consistent with many forms of *Theosis* in Eastern theology.

A third expansion of theological thought is evident in Torrance's extension of the "hypostatic union" from a particular Christological formulation to a universal formulation attempting to explain the union of God and all human beings in Jesus' incarnation.

Throughout the history of Christian doctrinal thought the "hypostatic union" has referred only to the union of deity and humanity in the singular Person of Jesus Christ. It is certainly questionable whether the statement of "hypostatic union" that came out of the Council of Chalcedon necessary allows for or leads to the expanded conclusions that T.F. Torrance draws in his distinctive theology system. It seems to me that the theological thought of Torrance goes beyond the intent of the church thinkers in the early centuries, particularly those of the 4th and 5th centuries.

Many have observed that the theology of TFT is not traditional, orthodox Christian teaching. It is a theological *novum*, a novelty not observed in Christian theology until the twentieth century, despite the attempts of TFT and his interpreters to find allusion to such ideas in prior Christian thought.

## Particular Nuances of T.F. Torrance's Thought

Torrance keys off of the Chalcedonian formulation of the "hypostatic union," and postulates that there is a double movement within the divine-human "hypostatic union." This thesis of double movement (itself an expansion of Chalcedonian thought) is explained by TFT as (1) God's action toward man; the God-ward to man-ward divine action of redemption. (2) Man's action toward God; the man-ward to God-ward response to God's redemptive action in Jesus Christ. Torrance proceeds to explain that that Jesus, the God-man, embodies in Himself all of the double movement action in both directions in His own divine-human being.

This double-movement thesis sets up a central feature of the Torrance theology, the assertion that all of God's redemptive and saving action is essentially effected in the incarnation of Jesus. This is what was referred to earlier as the thesis of "incarnational atonement."

TF Torrance's theological system might be termed a "front-loaded" theological paradigm. Torrance emphasizes the incarnation of Jesus over the crucifixion. The entirety of God's saving action of mankind is in the incarnation. Though Paul said, "We preach Christ crucified" (I Cor. 1:23), the new kerygmatic emphasis of Torrance might be, "We preach Christ incarnated as the Man standing in as all men, and taking all men into unity with God."

Torrance regards the cross as a hidden, ineffable mystery and suggests that we should not presume to enclose the mystery of the atonement in human words or doctrinal formulations. "We can never reduce the act of God at

Calvary to any mere 'theory' of atonement." (TFT, *Atonement*, 3,4), this despite that fact that his own theology proffers such a theory of atonement – a unique and original one, at that.

TFT's theological focus was not on the cross or the death of Jesus Christ. The cross is viewed as a concluding event that wraps up the incarnational action. The cross is just the finalization of the undoing of Adam. When Jesus died on the cross, he put the flesh of Adam to death. Adamic humanity is laid to rest and buried. Adamic existence within mankind is terminated.

But the early Christians did not seem to focus on the incarnation of Jesus. They celebrated Christ's crucifixion, resurrection, ascension and Pentecost. They did not even celebrate Christmas until hundreds of years later, beginning in the 4th century after Emperor Constantine's mother, Helena, went to Palestine and claimed to have discovered the birthplace of Jesus in Bethlehem.

It is legitimate to conclude that Torrance's front-loaded theology that puts all the weight and importance on the incarnation rather than on the death, resurrection, ascension, and Pentecostal outpouring, moves beyond the parameters of traditional Christian teaching through the centuries.

Another nuance of Torrance's theological thought also connects with his "incarnational atonement" extension of the Chalcedonian "hypostatic union" of deity and humanity. TFT advocated that when the Son of God became human in the God-man, Jesus assumed the *sinful* human nature and flesh of fallen human in order to heal our humanity by means of recreation, recapitulation and reconciliation.

The reasoning for this feature of TFT's theology is his acceptance of the Augustinian understanding of human composition (the dualism of body and soul), and the essential corruption that the fall of Adam effected upon all humankind. TFT emphasized that it was the "*sinful* human nature and flesh of fallen humanity" that Jesus assumed in the incarnation. Why was this an important point to Torrance? Because he repetitively quoted the statement of Gregory of Nazianzus that "the unassumed is the unhealed." If Jesus did not assume *sinful* humanness, then He did not heal *sinful* humanness. The text used to support this thesis is "God sent His Son *in the likeness of sinful flesh*..." (Rom. 8:3).

Torrance's anthropological presuppositions colored his Christological and soteriological positions. Taking the problematic reference to "*sinful* flesh" in Rom. 8:3, TFT utilizes the Augustinian supposition of the intrinsic sinfulness of humanness, connecting this premise with the thesis of Jesus' "vicarious humanity" in the place of every man, he conjectures the humanity of Jesus to be ontologically connected to the being of all humanity in such a way that the humanity of Jesus can recreate humanity from its sinful, fallen condition to a divine-human condition. Jesus assumed our fallen flesh from Mary; He sanctified our human nature in the very act of incarnational assumption, and all through His Life He lived it from the beginning to the end in His "vicarious humanity."

 All that God desired to do and accomplish for mankind is completed objectively, and "already realized" in the hypostatic union of divine and human natures in Jesus Christ, according to TFT.

The foundational Torrance thesis of "Vicarious humanity" implies that Jesus became divine-human being "in place of" all mankind. This seems to be a new form of replacement theology. TFT explains that Jesus Christ acted/acts "as man, in the place of all men." He takes our place and represents us, so that what is true of Him is true of us, and what He did in His humanity is applicable and attributable to all human beings.

The thesis of the "vicarious humanity" of Jesus Christ becomes the organizing tenet of Christian Christology and soteriology in Torrance's theology. This is the distinctive introduced as a theological *novum* by the Torrance brothers. Piggybacking on the theology of Karl Barth, the Swiss theologian, (who both Torrance brothers studied under as a theological mentor), and his emphasis on the incarnation as the point where "God became flesh," subsuming all humanity into a reconciled union with God, to the extent that he (Barth) could entitle a book, *The Humanity of God*, the Torrance brothers carried the Barthian theology of Christology over into the realm of soteriology (the doctrine of salvation) by emphasizing the "vicarious humanity" of Jesus, whereby Jesus was regarded as "the Man for all men," the substitute and replacement of/for every human being. Jesus becomes the "Master-man," not just "the Man *for* all men," but "the Man *as* (in place of) all man," who represents, stands in the stead of, replaces all humanity henceforth from the incarnation forward (and backwards).

Christian theology has long explained that Jesus' death was a "vicarious" or substitutional death on behalf of all humanity. This has been exegetically documented by scripture verses that refer to Jesus' death "for" us or "on our behalf." The prepositions used in those scripture verses are usually *huper* or *anti*, and they predominantly clarify the intended action of the verb "to die." The vicariousness of Jesus action "on our behalf" is primarily (if not exclusively) explaining the purpose of the atoning crucifixion death of Jesus Christ on the Cross of Calvary. But

TFT extends that to apply to the entire life of Jesus' alleged "vicarious humanity."

Torrance has taken the liberty to extend this concept of substitution or vicariousness to the incarnation and the entire life of Jesus. In the process, he has invested the prepositions with a questionable connotation of "in the place of," or "in the stead of." Though these may be possible translations of the prepositions, they are not the primary usage. Some lexicographers question or deny whether either of these prepositions should legitimately carry the connotation of *replacement.*

The "vicarious humanity" thesis is a novelty introduced into Christian theology by the Torrance brothers, with questionable biblical support and questionable theological precedence.

Despite T.F. Torrance's citation of early church sources, these do not necessarily support his thesis of "vicarious humanity." He reads into them (*eisegesis* – just like he does the scriptures) what he wants to see, and then uses them as documenting sources. One has to admit, though, that the early church literature probably does make more use of the incarnation than has been seen in evangelical theology for the past couple of centuries.

It is Torrance's assertion that in the hypostatic union of His own person, Jesus effected an ontological exchange whereby sinful human "being" was exchanged for the divine-human "being" of Jesus in all human beings. Henceforth, human beings have no ontological existence apart from the "ontological solidarity" God has established with us in the hypostatic union of God and humanity in Jesus Christ. All human beings, without exception, are ontologically bound up in the incarnate reality of Jesus

19

Christ, and are already redeemed, resurrected, and consecrated for the glory of God.

As a result, according to Torrance's theological system, the reconciliation or "at-one-ment" of God and all humanity was effected in the divine-human union of Jesus' incarnation and His "vicarious humanity." The primary text that TFT uses to support this contention is II Cor. 5:19 – "God was in Christ reconciling the world to Himself."

**Objective action of divine redemption and atonement effected by means of the incarnation of Jesus Christ**

The aforementioned theological premises of TFT provide the stepping-stones by which he applies every act of Jesus to all of humanity. The Pauline explanation that the Son of God "emptied Himself, taking the form of a bondservant, being made in the likeness of men" (Phil. 2:7) is given a unique interpretation by TFT. The kenotic "emptying" of the Son of God is understood to be His Self-humiliation of becoming humanity, the Man as all men. This is conjoined with the biblical concept of "ransom." "The Son of man came to give His life a ransom for many" (Matt. 20:28; Mk. 10:45; I Tim. 2:6). The Son "emptied Himself" to become the incarnated "ransom" for all humanity.

The "righteous act" that Paul referred to in Romans 5:18 – "through one act of righteousness there resulted justification of life to all men" – is understood by Torrance to be the "righteous act" of Jesus' willingness to become humanity, rather than the traditional explanation of His willingness to die on behalf of all men.

Paul's expression that God "made Him who knew no sin to be sin on our behalf, so that we might become the righteousness of God in Him" (I Cor. 5:21) is likewise reinterpreted by TFT to mean that Jesus was "made to be sin" in assuming "*sinful* flesh" in the incarnation.

Paul's words that "God sent His own Son in the likeness of sinful flesh, and as an offering for sin, He condemned sin in the flesh" (Rom. 8:3), is also interpreted to mean that by His incarnation, Jesus "condemned sin in the flesh," rather than the historically accepted explanation that it was by His offering of death for sin on the cross was the action of condemning sin in the flesh.

Whereas Paul's words, "You have been bought with a price" (I Cor. 6:20; 7:23), have traditionally been understood by explaining the "price paid" for the sins of mankind was Jesus' death on the cross, TFT recasts the meaning to the "price was paid" in Jesus' assumption of humanity.

These are but a sampling of the manner by which T.F. Torrance completely reinterprets the events of Jesus' life within the paradigm of the "vicarious humanity" of Jesus and His alleged incarnational atonement.

## Subjective response of man is performed objectively and vicariously "in our place" by Jesus.

Previous note was made of Torrance's assertion of the two-fold movement that he regarded to be intrinsic to the "hypostatic union" – the God-ward to man-ward movement, as well as the man-ward to God-ward movement. We now turn our attention to TFT's explanation of how all human response to God's action in the Son has been performed objectively and vicariously "in our place" by Jesus.

According to TFT, all objective and subjective realities were fulfilled once-for-all in the incarnate constitution of Jesus Christ, and are in no wise dependent upon a believer's personal decision of faith.

In his own words, Torrance writes:

> "The incarnate Word yielded the 'perfect response of man' to the divine revelation He himself embodied. We are not concerned simply with a divine revelation which demands from us all a human response, but with a divine revelation which already includes a true and appropriate and fully human response as part of its achievement for us and to us and in us." (TFT, *Theology. In Reconstruction* 129-132)

> "Jesus Christ himself IS the perfect human response to God. He is both the divine Word of God spoken to humanity and, at the same time, the perfect human word addressed to God" (TFT, *God & Rationality*)

> "In Jesus Christ, God has not only condescended to 'objectify" himself so that man may know him, but also has provided from the side of man, and from within man, 'adequate and perfect reception' of the truth of divine revelation. (TFT *Theological Science.* 50)

> "the whole life and activity of Jesus from the cradle to the grave constitutes the vicarious human response which God has graciously and unconditionally provided for us" (TFT, *Mediation of Christ*, 79)

> "Jesus Christ is our human response to God (TFT, *Mediation of Christ*, 80)

In the thought of TFT the "vicarious humanity" of Jesus provides the manward-Godward movement of incarnational atonement – all of this inherent in Torrance's unique extension and expansion of the "hypostatic union."

The redemption of mankind is not achieved primarily by the death of Jesus, but by His life that He lived in our flesh as our replacement, and for our sakes. The text TFT cites for this premise is Rom. 5:10 – "we are saved by His life."

What we are seeing is that TFT regarded every action of Jesus to be an action in our place fulfilling all the basic acts of man's response to God: faith, repentance, obedience, prayer, the receiving of God's blessing, and even thankful gratitude for such.

The entirety of the Protestant explanation of "justification by faith" is reinterpreted in TFT's theology. Torrance explained, "Justification has been fulfilled subjectively as well as objectively in Jesus Christ, but that objective and subjective justification is *objective* to us. ...His subjective justification becomes ours...(TFT, *Justification* Scottish Journal of Theology, 225-246). Justification is subjectively realized in the vicarious humanity of Jesus Christ.

Torrance did not regard justification and sanctification to be sequential parts of an *ordo salutis*. He rejected the complete idea of an *ordo salutis* with its various subjective elements. His contention was that there is no "order of salvation" because salvation was singularly effected in the "hypostatic union" of the incarnation.

TFT rejected the Western theological propensity to separate and distinguish between divine grace and human freedom, regarding such to be another dualist construct. All divine and human actions are realized *in Christo*; they are intrinsic to Christ's incarnate assumption of fallen human life and the whole course of His filial obedience to the Father.

Torrance taught that every act of God and man was implemented  by God in the incarnation of Jesus, inclusive of every response that man should make to God's provision. Jesus provides for us not only the remission of sins, but makes us share in the positive righteousness of His obedient and saving life. Jesus stood "in our place" as The Believer, as The Obedient One. He "took our place" even in the acts of repentance and personal decision. TFT's premise of the "vicarious humanity" of Jesus involves the unification of all divine agency and human agency. In Jesus there was full divine and human agency, and the response to the gospel is comprehended in His fully divine and human agency.

Reacting to the *dualism* he perceived in any cooperative effort of salvation between God and man, and denying that man can do anything towards his own salvation, TFT overreacted by denying any response of man, leaving but the Augustinian determinism of divine action.

It will be instructive to focus a little closer on TFT's premise that Jesus was the faithful believer "in our place." A particular verse of scripture that he used to defend the theory of the "vicarious humanity" in the objectified-subjective response of man was Galatians 2:20. Paul wrote, "It is no longer I who lives, but Christ lives in me," a statement that Torrance interpreted as a vicarious replacement of Christ in the believer. This was extended to indicate that Christ lived in the believer in terms of his or her faith. The King James Version continues Gal. 2:20 with, "the life I now live I live by the faith *of* the Son of God..." This translation of the Greek genitive in the King James Bible conveniently coincided with TFT's premise.

In Torrance's own words, "Faith is not to be construed as an independent, autonomous act which arises from a base within ourselves" (TFT *Med. Of Christ*, 82). He goes on, "faith and belief do not properly describe a virtue or quality of human beings. Faith is intensely personalized in the incarnation of Jesus Christ. Christ is the incarnation of the divine *pistis*; He is the embodiment and actualization of

24

human *pistis*." "Jesus Christ is not only the incarnate Word of God; he is also the vicarious Believer for us. His very humanity is the embodiment of our salvation" (TFT *Expository Times*).

"Modern evangelism shares the gospel in an unevangelical manner. To say, 'This is what Jesus Christ has done for you, but you will not be saved unless you make your own personal decision for Christ as your Savior and give your heart to him – this is a form of 'conditional grace'". The Evangel has taken the place of us all."

So, to restate Torrance's position, Jesus Christ has already made a "personal decision of faith" in place of and on behalf of every one of us. We do not "accept the Lord" in order to be saved; He has already "accepted" us and included us in His High-priestly Self-offering to the Father. Evangelism is the invitation for hearers to become what they already are, i.e. to participate actively in the reality of the salvation that is already theirs in Jesus Christ. Jesus Christ was, and is, the Obedient Man "in our place, and the total obedience of Jesus' life is attributed to every human being.

In addition, it is the assertion of TFT that Jesus spoke to the Father in prayer "in our place," and worshipped God the Father "in our place." Even the prayer and worship of a Christian is regarded to be vicariously accomplished by the incarnate Jesus. As TFT puts it, "Jesus' Self-oblation to the Father IS our worship and prayer. Jesus Christ the Incarnated Son honors, worships and glorifies the Father in our place. Jesus makes Himself our prayer, and is the prayer in us, for we do not know how to pray as we ought (cf. Rom. 8:26). He is the vicarious worship and prayer with which we respond to the love of the Father." James B. Torrance, the brother of T.F. Torrance, explicitly articulated this thesis in his book, *Worship, Community, and the Triune God of Grace.*

25

The next assertion of how the "vicarious humanity" of Jesus is applied to all humanity is particularly shocking to most evangelicals. Torrance explained that Jesus effected regeneration (new birth) for all humanity when He was incarnated as an infant.

In his words, "The New Testament does not use the term regeneration (*paliggenesia*), as evangelical theology does, for what goes on in the human heart. It is used only of the great regeneration that took place in and through the Incarnation. Conversion or 'new birth,' does not apply to what happens in the heart of the individual believer, but to the regeneration of the human mind in the incarnation."

Elsewhere, Torrance explains "conversion" in this way: "The eternal Son assumes the sinful human mind and converts it back to the Father in a 'radical and complete *metanoia*." The explanation that this is a collective mind-conversion is quite different from the evangelical explanation of a spiritual conversion.

Read carefully TFT's explanation of regeneration:

"During my first week of office as Moderator of the General Assembly of the Church of Scotland when I presided at the Assembly's Gaelic Service, a highlander asked me whether I was born again, and when I replied in the affirmative he asked when I had been born again. I still recall his face when I told him that I had been born again when Jesus Christ was born of the Virgin Mary and rose again from the virgin tomb, the first-born from the dead. When he asked me to explain I said: 'This Tom Torrance you see is full of corruption, but the real Tom Torrance is hid with Christ in God and will be revealed only when Jesus comes again. He took my corrupt humanity in his Incarnation, sanctified, cleansed and redeemed it, giving it new birth, in his death and resurrection.' In other words, our new birth, our regeneration, our conversion, are what has taken place in Jesus Christ himself, so that when we speak of our conversion or our

26

regeneration we are referring to our sharing in the conversion or regeneration of our humanity brought about by Jesus in and through himself for our sake. In a profound and proper sense, therefore, we must speak of Jesus Christ as constituting in himself the very substance of our conversion, so that we must think of him as taking our place even in our acts of repentance and personal decision, for without him all so-called repentance and conversion are empty. Since a conversion in that truly evangelical sense is a turning away from ourselves to Christ, it calls for a conversion from our in-turned notions of conversion to one which is grounded and sustained in Christ Jesus himself."
– Thomas F. Torrance, *The Mediation of Christ*, New Ed. (Helmers & Howard, 1992), 85-86

It is obvious that Torrance's conception of "new birth," "regeneration" or "conversion" is such that it has taken place in Jesus Christ Himself for all mankind. Believers today simply share in the conversion or regeneration of our humanity brought about by Jesus in and through Himself for our sake.

Continuing to consider how the "vicarious humanity" of Jesus inclusively incorporates Jesus' every act "in place of" all actions for every human being, Jesus is also regarded as having received the Spirit of God on behalf of all humanity.

"In the incarnation, God is imparted to humanity by means of the Spirit, ... the Holy Spirit comes to dwell in humanity. God the Holy Spirit is mediated to mankind "by" and "through" the humanity of Jesus Christ. When the Holy Spirit descended upon Christ in the Jordan River, ...the Spirit's descent was a descent upon fallen humanity as assumed by the incarnate Son. When He received the Spirit, we received the Spirit" (TFT *Trinitarian Faith*, 190). In this manner Torrance interprets the meaning of the words, "the Holy Spirit has been poured out on all flesh" (Acts 2:17, cf. Joel 2:28).

In addition, Torrance contends that Jesus was baptized for all mankind. When Jesus was "washed" and baptized in the Jordan River, all of humanity was "washed" and baptized.

*Baptisma* does not refer to the baptizing of an individual, but rather to "the baptism with which Jesus Christ Himself was baptized for our sakes in the whole course of His redemptive life, from His birth to His resurrection." In the incarnation Jesus was overwhelmed and baptized with our humanity, baptized "as us." His whole life was a baptism for our sakes, as He received the baptism meant for sinners. The physical water baptism of individuals is but their 'initiation' into the vicarious *baptisma* of Jesus Christ, the one all-inclusive baptism common to Christ and His Church. The objective, once-for-all baptism (*baptisma*) of Jesus into humanity is the unrepeatable reality thereafter signified by the water rite in which individuals participate. Jesus' vicarious baptism with humanity in the incarnation is the objective truth of the "one baptism" of that Paul refers to in Eph. 4:5, "one Lord, one faith, one baptism."

Torrance even proceeds to indicate that Jesus gave thanks eucharistically "in the place of" all humanity. Jesus in Himself is the *sacramentum* of God, who makes visible the invisible realities of God.

"Our partaking of the bread and wine is not merely something we do to 'remember' Christ, but a 'communion' in His Eucharistic offering to the Father - the objective reality of Christ's Eucharistic 'real presence' from incarnation to ascension. We just participate in His self-consecration and self-offering of thanksgiving which He made in our place and on our behalf. ... The 'real presence' of Christ is not merely in the bread and wine but in the ontological identification of Jesus in our place. In His 'incarnate Person" He was the "body broken for us."

## Additional Theological Categories

Many readers may be completely baffled by TFT's universal inclusion of all humanity in the "vicarious humanity" of the Person of Jesus Christ, as implemented by the novel explanation of "incarnational atonement." Before we make any judgments concerning his theological interpretations, let us proceed to consider some general theological categories wherein Torrance's theological system seems to differ and diverge from traditional Christian teaching as most of us have known it. In that we have already been addressing Christological and soteriological categories, we shall consider some other categories.

*Theological Anthropology*

Despite T. F. Torrance's eagle-eye for spotting dualism in cosmological, epistemological and theological categories, and his particular exposure of dualism in the thought of Augustine, he seems to have had a blind-spot that made him oblivious to the obvious dualism in Augustine's theological anthropology – the body/soul dualism. In accord with Karl Barth, he refers to man as "an embodied soul," as well as "an ensouled body." TFT failed to challenge the Augustinian distortion of anthropological dualism, and thus could not restructure a much-needed Christian anthropology.

T.F. Torrance indicated that an "ontological exchange" was necessitated for fallen humanity. This is predicated on the Augustinian premise that "human nature" or "human being" was corrupted and ruined in the Fall of Adam. *Humanum*, humanness, was rendered deficient, defective, and depraved. If man was going to be man as God intended man to be, he would need an "exchange of being," his corrupted and ruined human nature or "being" would need to be exchanged for a new kind of "human being." In the incarnation, according to TFT, the Son of God became Man on behalf of all humanity, willing to thereby facilitate the exchange of His "divine-human being" for the "corrupted human being" of fallen mankind. Instead of Adamic human-being, all humanity would henceforth have Christic divine-human-being.

In T.F. Torrance's theological paradigm, fallen humanity did not have a spiritual problem, so spiritual exchange was not the solution! Humanity just needed a radical rehumanization to correct the dehumanization that occurred at the Fall in Adam. TFT refers to "the humanizing in Jesus of dehumanized man." Regeneration in the thought of TFT turns out to be rehumanization.

Human nature is alleged by TFT to be reconstituted by the "vicarious humanity" of Jesus. In support of this thesis Torrance often quoted Irenaeus' comment about the "recapitulation of humanity." Sin-compromized humanity, as a whole, is assumed by Jesus, according to TFT. Often quoting the phrase of Gregory of Nazianzus, "the unassumed is the unhealed," Torrance drew the conclusion that in the assumption of humanity all humanity is healed.

His thesis that Jesus Christ as Man replaces all mankind, effectively obliterates all individuated human beings. Humanity is collectively considered "in Christ." All sense of individuality is incorporated into the collective consideration of humanity as a whole.

*Diabology – Satanology – Evil*

There are very few references to Satan or the devil in T.F. Torrance's writings, but there are numerous vague references to evil and the forces that counter God.

Reacting against the perceived dualism of casting God and Satan in conflict, TFT seems to have followed Karl Barth in positing a "non-ontological realist" view of the devil, demons, and evil in general, denying them ontological substance. Positing that all "Being" and "personhood" are in God, evil becomes but godless emptiness that only exists as negativity or nothingness, the *nihil*. That which stands in opposition to God is defined by absence or privation. Death, sin, the devil are regarded as but the vacuum of what is not God. Satan has no spiritual, personal, ontological "being." He is regarded as a negative, unintelligible, non-personal dynamic or force of evil, that reacts, opposes and rebels against what God is doing in Jesus Christ. He has no real being, no real power, and no real influence. Satan is relegated to a non-entity; just a nebulous, negative "force" of evil.

Such a non-ontological, non-personal presence of evil could not "prowl like a roaring lion" (I Pet. 5:8), malevolently scheming against man (Eph. 6:11), and tempting human beings (Matt. 4:1-3; I Thess. 3:5). TFT would certainly not conceive of Satan as "the spirit that works in the sons of disobedience" (Eph. 2:2), so that the whole world of fallen mankind "lies in the Evil One' (I Jn. 5:19), and are identified with "their father, the devil" (Jn. 5:20).

*Hamartiology – Sin*

Given the inexplicability of evil in Torrance's thought, sin is likewise an ambiguous non-reality. TFT states, "God does not offer us any explanation for evil, but deals decisively and finally with it by entering himself into its abysmal chasm separating us from him and bridging it through the atoning life and death of his incarnate Son." (*The Mediation of Christ*, xiv). Evil involves a radical discontinuity that cannot be explained. The "abysmal irrationality of evil" required nothing less that the hypostatic union.

31

T.F. Torrance's expansion of the hypostatic union focuses on the "onto-relational" union of God and man in Jesus Christ, casting sin as the "impossible possibility" of a fatal contradiction in our relationship with God. Sin is but the negativity of the human personhood that God intends for man. The fall of man into sin effected an ontological, constitutional change in human nature, causing the unthinkable irrationality of sin to be regarded as intrinsic to fallen humanity. By the union of divinity and humanity in Jesus Christ, God penetrates to the ontological depths of our being, and ontologically replaces our corrupt and sinful human being with the divine-human being of Jesus Christ. Jesus' hypostatic union penetrated into the perverted structures of human existence and reversed the process of corruption, and saved us from perdition.

Torrance's mentor, Karl Barth, spoke of "the unfruitful knowledge of sin, evil, death, and the devil," indicating that these are impossible to understand except as they are overcome in the revelation of God in Christ. In other words, we can only understand the depravity of man in the light of God's grace in Jesus Christ, by understanding sin as the contrasted deprivation of divine righteousness.

*Pistology – the study of belief and faith*

TFT continues the Augustinian attribution of "faith as the gift of God," but the novelty of his teaching is that such faith is not granted arbitrarily to divinely elected individuals, but collectively to all humanity in the vicarious subjectivity of the faithful actions of the historical life of Jesus Christ, extended to humanity in all ages. Instead of faith being the response of man to God's provision in Jesus Christ, faith is regarded as the "gift of God" given to all humanity by the "vicarious humanity" of Jesus Christ. In Jesus' subjective faithfulness, He is alleged to have exercised faith on behalf of, in the place of, and as a substitute for, all individual human beings. This "faith of Christ" attributed to all mankind is explained by using the genitive of Galatians 2:20 to refer to Christ's faith as does the King James Bible translation of the English Bible.

Human exercise of faith by an individual is regarded as but a cognitive awareness that overcomes one's erroneous thinking about not being included in the extension of Christ's hypostatic union to all mankind.

TFT retains the Augustinian/Calvinist concept of "unconditional election," extending the premise to a strictly Theonomous approach of God's control over the entire process of all interaction between God and man. The classic "limited atonement" thesis intrinsic to Augustinian/ Calvinist thought has been rejected by Torrance, and some of his followers opt instead for an "unlimited atonement" reconciling all mankind to God, thus opening their thought to the charge of universalism. Others take a more cautious approach seeking to preserve the concept of "limited atonement" by limiting the reconciling oneness between God and man to the Person of Jesus Christ, wherein all of humanity are objectively and subjectively brought inclusively into union with God.

*Pneumatology – the Spirit*

With no awareness of the human spirit, due to the soul/body dualism of man's anthropological function, and thus no understanding of the derivative spiritual function of human beings, it is no wonder that there is little emphasis on pneumatology, on the *pneumatikoi* of spiritual realities in the theology of TFT.

Torrance's theology is practically devoid of any emphasis on the indwelling presence of the Spirit of God, the Spirit of Christ, the Holy Spirit in the human spirit of an individual.

His dualistic anthropology allowed only for the "body and soul" differentiations, so it is quite understandable that there is no deliberation of the indwelling presence of the Spirit within the human spirit. The internal spiritual realities that evangelicals have referred to as a "personal relationship with Jesus Christ" are rather foreign to TFT's thought.

The subjective interiority of the gospel in the receptive individual Christian is missing in TFT's theology. The inner subjective realities of personal relationship are "objectified" into the experience of Jesus serving as our "vicarious humanity." This becomes an objectified "universal subjective" whereby human subjectivity is objectively replaced by the vicarious human experience of Jesus Christ. The human subjective is not individuated in personal inner spiritual realities, but is objectified to the personal "subjective" actions of Jesus Christ, both historically and contemporaneously.

His theology wipes out all meaning of an individual human's subjective response to Jesus Christ. All internal spiritual realities of individual experience and relationship with the living Lord Jesus are incorporated into the objectified recapitulation of humanity via the incarnated "vicarious humanity" of Jesus.

*Bibliology – Scripture*

The theological enterprise of T.F. Torrance is basically a philosophical theology, rather than a Biblical theology. Such an approach does not necessitate or call for precision of scriptural documentation of what is presented.

Torrance explains his approach in these words: "The humanity of Jesus, the incarnate Word of God, that is the "real text" underlying the New Testament. The scriptures cannot be abstracted from the Son of God incarnate in history and made, in themselves, the object of independent investigation, as occurred in post-Reformation Scholasticism, when the words of scripture were elevated to the status of "the truth" and detached from Jesus Christ. Jesus Christ IS the Word of God. The Bible must not be reduced to a collection of propositional truths, abstracted and considered apart from the Word of God incarnate in the person of Jesus Christ."

TFT minimized the commonly accepted "historical/ grammatical" basis of exegesis and hermeneutics. Instead, he advocated what he termed "theological depth exegesis" – using the grid of his extrapolated interpretation of *homoousion* and "hypostatic union" in order to interpret scripture as a whole. Scripture was to be read eisegetically through the lens of his theological understanding.

*Trinitarian Theology*

We would be totally remiss in our analysis and critique of the theology of T.F. Torrance if we did not conclude with the area of his theological thought that should rightfully be identified and elevated as the most groundbreaking contribution to Christian thought in recent centuries. He will certainly and most legitimately be remembered as a foremost "Theologian of the Trinity" during the twentieth century.

His concentration on, and reconfiguring of Christian thought concerning the distinctive of the Triune Being of God came in the latter stages of his life. This was due in part to the academic restrictions imposed by his being Professor of Christian Dogmatics at New College, University of Edinburgh. The Scottish higher education system limited the seminary to instruction of the dogma of the Church, but philosophical consideration of God (theology proper) was the domain of the department of philosophy. So, it was after his tenure in the department of theological dogmatics at Edinburgh, that TFT had the time and freedom to pursue his studies of the Christian perspective of God as Trinity.

It was Torrance's contention that much of the history of Christian theological thought about God incorporated the substantialist metaphysics of Greek philosophical thought. Plato's *a priori* methodology, in particular, projected and postulated essential or substantial categories as comprising the Being of the ultimate Reality. Early Christian thinkers followed this line of thinking by projecting idealized superlatives such as eternal, infinite, invisible, immutable, perfect and supreme as the constituency of the divine Being.

T.F. Torrance took the argument of the essential ontology of God back to the expressions of the "Cappadocian Fathers" at the Council of Constantinople (A.D. 381), and their argument that the interpersonal communion and fellowship of the three Persons of the Godhead, Father, Son, and Holy Spirit was the basis of understanding the essential Being of the Triune God. Rather than the Greek conception of substantialist categories serving as the constructs of God's Being, Torrance insisted that the unique Christian concept of the Triune God must necessarily be formed in a "revealed theology" that was founded on the Self-revelation of God in the Son and by the Spirit. The relational metaphysics of the ontological relations of the three Persons of the Triune God must serve as the Christian understanding of the essential Being of God instead of the substantialist metaphysics of Greek philosophy. Such an onto-relational Trinitarian recognition of the divine *ousia* (Being), Torrance maintained, serves as the foundational divine dynamic of all interpersonal relationships.

Much of the theology of TFT will likely be challenged and debated in Christian circles for decades, if not centuries, but the redirection of Trinitarian thought from the Hellenic philosophical categories to an emphasis on the Self-revelation of God in the Son, Jesus Christ, and the recognition that the ontological understanding of God's Being must be formulated by the personal relationality of the Trinity should stand out as the shining star of Torrance's contribution to Christian thought and be given due consideration for centuries to come.

Any Christian interested in a deeper academic understanding of this important and distinctive tenet of Christian thought, the essential Triunity of God, would be well served to read T.F. Torrance's books *The Trinitarian Faith* (1988), *Trinitarian Perspectives* (1994), and The *Christian Doctrine of God: One Being Three Persons* (1996). These will be standard texts for Christian theology students for decades to come.

**CONCLUSION**

The preceding synopsis of the theology of T.F. Torrance will give way to the author's personal appraisal of the same in these concluding comments.

Coming as he does, from the Reformed theological formation of his Scottish Presbyterian background, and serving in that context for most of his professional life, Torrance perpetuates the classic Protestant tendency to over-objectify the action of Jesus Christ, and to diminish emphasis on the subjective inwardness of Jesus' function as the "life-giving Spirit" (I Cor. 15:45) in individual Christian lives. For Torrance, the traditional subjective elements of Christian faith are objectified in the "vicarious humanity" of Jesus – subsumed into objective categories that create a rather oxymoronic "objectified-subjectivity." By means of this subsumption of personal subjective response into the objective and vicarious action of Jesus, TFT establishes a "universal subjective" wherein all personal response is allegedly included in Jesus' subjective actions, and regarded as objectively and universally applied to all humanity. The entire Christian emphasis of "personal relationship" with God through Christ is diminished or sacrificed. The personal relationality of God and human individuals is objectified in abstract logical terms, rather than in genuine personal relationships. TFT's distinctive emphasis on onto-relationalism becomes but an academic exercise.

Torrance's theological explorations, as a whole, tended to be cerebral academic forays into philosophical theology, crafted with careful rational complexity. He employs a great deal of historical theology, albeit colored by his theological presuppositions, but the bulk of his endeavors pertain to philosophical theology, rather than biblical theology.

Rather than the Son of God assuming the form of an individual human in the person of Jesus Christ, as has been the traditional and orthodox explanation of the hypostatic union since Chalcedon, Torrance seems to develop a form of "subsumption theology," that involves a deterministic subsumption of all humanity into the Person and action of Jesus Christ. The whole of humanity is subsumed either into the Christ-person and His work or into the essence of deity. The precursor for this concept of subsumption was evidenced in Karl Barth's book, *The Humanity of God*.

By centering his entire theological paradigm in the Person and work of Jesus Christ, Torrance does develop a very Christocentric theological system. For this he should be applauded, as Jesus must be the primary issue of Christian thought. His methodology of emphasizing the life and work of Jesus Christ to the exclusion of all human response has, however, opened his theological system to the charge of

Christomonism, implying a reduction of all theology to Christology. This charge was also applied to his mentor, Karl Barth, and in both cases seems to have some legitimacy.

In his rejection of the classic Augustinian/Calvinist tenet of "limited atonement" and the thesis of the divine selection of particular individuals to receive the benefits of the redemptive efforts of Jesus Christ, Torrance apparently sought to avoid the rigid determinism of that theological system that he had inherited. But in failing to jettison the accompanying tenet of "unconditional election," the premise of divine determinism remains foundational to TFT's system of theological thought. Thought not limited to individuated selection, such determinism is now expanded to the universal inclusion of all humanity.

When the novel theological premise of the "vicarious humanity" of Jesus in place of all humanity is applied to Christian thought, in conjunction with the denial of individuated human response to the Person and work of Jesus Christ, the inevitable outcome is a system of thought that veers toward deterministic universalism. Torrance denied that his thought was a form of universalism, and a technical loophole of logic seems to support that denial for the strict definition of absolute universalism is the contention that every human person will have an inevitable destiny in heaven. T.F. Torrance did not advocate such a wholesale universal inclusion, but his premise of the universal inclusion of humanity in the "vicarious humanity" of Jesus, alongside of his apparent denial of the personal individuated acceptance and reception of Jesus by an individual in order to engage in a personal relationship and experience with Jesus, effectively establishes a system of thought that leads in the direction of deterministic universalism.

T.F. Torrance's unique theses of the all-embracing "vicarious humanity" of Jesus and the all-encompassing theological implications of Jesus' incarnational restoration of humanity in his expansion of the hypostatic union constitute, despite his citations of Irenaeus, Athanasius, and the Cappadocians, a theological *novum* hitherto unknown in Christian theological thought. Such novelty should not, in itself, cause Christian readers and thinkers to question the orthodoxy of TFT's theological interpretations. Much less should we be inclined, as some have already done, to hurl epithets of "heresy" at Torrance's thought. Despite the innovation of his thought, and its divergence from historic and traditional Christian explanation, we must remember that the history of Christian thought and doctrine is replete with a variety of different ideologies necessitating Christian people to "agree to disagree" on many issues and interpretations.

In particular it should be noted that various atonement theories attempting to explain the redemptive and restorative work of Jesus Christ have emerged throughout the history of Christian thought. Examples of such are the ransom theory, the scapegoat theory, the satisfaction theory, the penal-substitution theory, the moral-influence theory, the governmental theory, the recapitulation theory, the *Christus Victor* theory, etc., all of which seem to have some scriptural support. For the most part, these various interpretations focused on the redemptive efficacy of the death of Christ and explained the reconciling atonement of God and man from the event of the crucifixion. The novelty of Torrance's theory of "incarnational atonement" is that he places the redemptive emphasis on the birth of Jesus rather than the death, and by his thesis of the "vicarious humanity" of Jesus inclusively encompasses all of humanity in the efficacy of the hypostatic being of the Person of Jesus.

My personal appraisal of T.F. Thomas is that despite my disagreement with much of his theological thought, as obviated in this document, my personal recollections of Tom Torrance are of a distinctly godly man and Christian brother in Christ. On every occasion that I was in his company, he exhibited the character of Christ, i.e. the "fruit of the Spirit" (Gal. 5:22,23). "By their fruit, you shall know them" (Matt. 7:20).

How will T.F. Torrance be adjudged by the Christian theological community as they contend with his thought in the future? Many have accepted his theological premises and are teaching such in colleges and seminaries. The Evangelical branch of Christian theology that emphasizes an individuated subjective response to the gospel will likely reject Torrance's thought, but would be well-advised to give due consideration to the objective-universal implications of Christ's Person and work that TFT emphasized, and most certainly need to consider the Trinitarian foundations of the Christian faith that he so carefully articulated.

The influence of the thought of T.F. Torrance will be dealt with in the theological community for decades, maybe centuries, to come. He will, no doubt, be recognized as a foremost "theologian of the Trinity," and will likely be identified as a "theologian of the incarnation and hypostatic union," since those themes dictate the whole of his theological system.

# Books by Thomas F. Torrance

- *The Doctrine of Grace in the Apostolic Fathers*. Edinburgh: Oliver & Boyd, 1948
- *Calvin's Doctrine of Man*. London: Lutterworth Press, 1949.
- *Kingdom and Church: A Study in the Theology of the Reformation*, Edinburgh: Oliver & Boyd, 1956.
- *When Christ Comes and Comes Again*. London: Hodder & Stoughton, 1957.
- *The Apocalypse Today*. Grand Rapids: Eerdmans, 1959.
- *Conflict and Agreement in the Church, I: Order and Disorder*. London: Lutterworth Press, 1959.
- *Conflict and Agreement in the Church, II: The Ministry and Sacraments of the Gospel*. London: Lutterworth Press, 1960.
- *Karl Barth: an Introduction to his Early Theology, 1910-1931*. London: SCM Press; New York: Harper & Row, 1962.
- *Theology in Reconstruction*. London: SCM Press Ltd, 1965.
- *Space, Time and Incarnation*. London: Oxford University Press, 1969
- *Theological Science*. London: Oxford University Press, 1969.
- *God and Rationality*. London: Oxford University Press, 1971.
- *Theology in Reconciliation: Essays towards Evangelical and Catholic Unity in East and West*. London: Geoffrey Chapman, 1975.
- *Space, Time and Resurrection*. Edinburgh: Handsel Press, 1976
- *The Ground and Grammar of Theology*. Charlottesville: The University Press of Virginia, 1980.
- *Divine and Contingent Order*. Oxford and New York: Oxford University Press, 1981.
- *The Incarnation: Ecumenical Studies in the Nicene-Constantinopolitan Creed*. Edinburgh: The Handsel Press, 1981.
- *Reality and Evangelical Theology*. Philadelphia: The Westminster Press, 1982.
- *Transformation & Convergence in the Frame of Knowledge: Explorations in the Interrelations of Scientific and Theological Enterprise*. Belfast: Christian Journals; Grand Rapids, MI: William B. Eerdmans, 1984.
- *The Christian Frame of Mind*. Edinburgh: Handsel Press, 1985
- *Reality and Scientific Theology* . The Margaret Harris Lectures, Dundee, 1970 (*Theology and Science at the Frontiers of Knowledge, vol 1*). Edinburgh: Scottish University Press, 1985
- *The Hermeneutics of John Calvin*. Edinburgh: Scottish Academic Press, 1988.
- *The Trinitarian Faith: The Evangelical Theology of the Ancient Catholic Church*. Edinburgh: T & T Clark, 1988.
- *Karl Barth, Biblical and Evangelical Theologian*. Edinburgh: T & T Clark, 1990.

- *The Mediation of Christ.* Colorado Springs: Helmers & Howard, 1992.
- *Royal Priesthood: A Theology of Ordained Ministry.* Edinburgh: T & T Clark, 1993.
- *Trinitarian Perspectives: Toward Doctrinal Agreement.* Edinburgh: T & T Clark, 1994.
- *Preaching Christ Today: The Gospel and Scientific Thinking.* Grand Rapids, MI: Eerdmans, 1994.
- *Divine Meaning: Studies in Patristic Hermeneutics.* Edinburgh: T & T Clark, 1995.
- *The Christian Doctrine of God, One Being Three Persons.* Edinburgh: T & T Clark, 1996.
- *Scottish Theology: From John Knox to John McLeod Campbell.* Edinburgh: T & T Clark, 1996.
- *Theological and Natural Science.* Eugene, Oregon: Wipf and Stock, 2002.
- *The Doctrine of Jesus Christ.* Eugene Oregon: Wipf and Stock Publishers, 2002.
- *Incarnation: The Person and Life of Christ.* Edited by Robert T. Walker. Downers Grove, Illinois: InterVarsity Press, 2008.
- *Atonement: The Person and Work of Christ.* Edited by Robert T. Walker. Downers Grove, Illinois: InterVarsity Press, 2009.